Flexible and Stuck Thinking

Ice Cream Shop Adventure

Think Social Publishing, Inc., Santa Clara, California
www.socialthinking.com

Flexible and Stuck Thinking
Ice Cream Shop Adventure

Ryan Hendrix, Kari Zweber Palmer, Nancy Tarshis, Michelle Garcia Winner

ISBN: 978-1-936943-30-2 (print)
ISBN: 978-1-936943-78-4 (ebook)

Think Social Publishing, Inc.
404 Saratoga Avenue, Suite 200
Santa Clara, CA 95050
Tel: (408) 557-8595
Fax: (408) 557-8594

This book was printed and bound in the United States by Mighty Color Printing.
TSP is a sole source provider of Social Thinking Products in the U.S.
Books may be purchased online at www.socialthinking.com.

Introduction to Storybook ⑧

The social world is complex; it shifts and changes constantly. Therefore to meet our own social goals, we shift and change with it. We are constantly learning how to be flexible, even throughout our adult lives.

Flexible thinking has to do with being able to engage in a variety of thoughts or experiences while acknowledging that many different paths could get us to our desired destination.

Stuck thinking can happen when we only consider one point of view. It can also be a result of missing information or over-focusing on details. It can be impacted by difficulty imagining alternatives or coming up with new ideas.

We Thinkers! Our Amazing Early Learner Curriculum!

We Thinkers! Volume 1* - *Social Explorers* and Volume 2 - *Social Problem Solvers* is an engaging Social Thinking® series designed to teach Michelle Garcia Winner's basic Social Thinking Vocabulary concepts to children ages 4-7. Each volume consists of storybooks, curricula and kid-friendly music that make core social concepts come alive for young learners. The teaching is cumulative: Volume 1 helps prime students for the deeper social concepts and activities in Volume 2.

Volume 1 explores five basic social concepts that help children learn about the social world around them, and, to observe and think about others as they learn to be part of a group: *thinking thoughts and feeling feelings, the group plan, thinking with your eyes, body in the group, and listening with brain and body.* Volume 2 introduces five core Social Thinking concepts related to teaching stronger executive functioning in a classroom or group setting: *hidden rules and expected/unexpected behavior, making a smart guess, flexible versus stuck thinking, the size of the problem, and sharing an imagination.* Each storybook is aligned with a curriculum unit that breaks down these social emotional concepts into concrete, teachable segments. Adults find detailed strategies and explicit ways to engage students and foster deeper learning about each concept.

Our goal in developing the *We Thinkers!* series is to provide sequenced clear instruction to engage students in their own social emotional learning so they can become better group collaborators and problem solvers. To that end, in Volume 2 we introduce a Group Collaboration, Play and Problem Solving (GPS) scale, checklist and interactive play activities. These materials guide parents and professionals in evaluating each child's current abilities to relate to their peers and then choose from an array of interactive play activities based on their particular social learning needs.

While all children can benefit from the social emotional teaching that is at the foundation of our *We Thinkers!* series, it was specifically designed to help promote social learning in neurotypical or neurodivergent children who also have social learning differences (e.g. autism spectrum levels 1 and 2, ADHD, social communication differences or social anxiety, etc. or no diagnoses). However, mainstream teachers now adopt our materials for use with all students as they find them user-friendly for all.

* formerly titled *The Incredible Flexible You, Volume 1*

Teaching the Curriculum, Concepts and Activities

What does play have to do with group collaboration and classroom learning? It is well documented in the research that interactive and pretend play is the avenue through which our young children practice and grow their social thinking and social skills. By the time children enter kindergarten it is assumed they have learned basic concepts and skills that allow them to work and learn academic concepts in a group setting.

It's tempting to think of play as simple, but it's actually a highly complex array of concepts and skills that work together simultaneously to enable a child to be successful in playing and interacting with others. Through interactive play children learn pivotal group interaction skills that will carry them through to adulthood. Play encourages the development of problem solving and conflict resolution skills, facilitates big-picture thinking, conceptual development, perspective taking, and executive functioning.

Our multi-sensory curriculum reflects the idea that learning should be interactive and playful. Activities involve using our eyes, ears, body and brain to make important social emotional connections. Teaching within the series draws on:

- "bibliotherapy" – using the words and illustrations in storybooks to help young learners develop an understanding of self and others and elicit a therapeutic response;

- "music therapy" – using music to help foster engagement around our core social emotional concepts;

- a wide range of activities to encourage children to explore and practice each of our 10 core concepts;

- "differentiated interactive play instruction" – not all children have the same abilities to play with other children. Through our GPS scale and checklist, parents and professionals can select which play activities are best suited to the child's level.

Together, the materials provided in our *We Thinkers!* series help young learners develop the five core competencies at the heart of social and emotional learning (SEL): self-awareness, self-management, social awareness, relationship skills, and responsible decision-making. The concepts marry playful, interactive learning to Common Core, state or country standards of education around the world.

Pace Yourself and Your Kids!

The concepts in Volume 2 explore group collaboration at a deeper level and the ideas are a little more detailed to teach. To increase engagement and protect kids from becoming overwhelmed, we recommend teaching the stories in sections. While we encourage you to let your students guide you in determining the "best" places to start and stop, we've noticed in our own teaching more natural breaking points in the plot and content. These sections are outlined below and are marked in the story.

Section 1, pages 1-5: Introduce the flexible and stuck thinking concepts

Section 2, pages 6-13: Examples of stuck thinking: going first, arguing over an idea, stuck on following one's own plan

Section 3, pages 14-21: Realizing the impact of stuck thinking; making a new plan using flexible thinking

Section 4, pages 22-31: Using flexible thinking to achieve a group goal

The *We Thinkers!* series is available for purchase in the U.S. at www.socialthinking.com.

Evan, Ellie, Jesse and Molly are working at an ice cream shop today.
The kids are all excited. It's so much fun to scoop ice cream,
take orders, and use the cash register!

The kids make a group plan. Everyone needs a job.
Evan says he will be the scooper. Ellie wants to answer
the phone, and Jesse will use the cash register.

2

Molly doesn't know what job she wants to do.

She sees a racecar through the front window. She brought her toy cars
and asks the kids if they want to play cars instead. They don't.

Molly's thoughts get stuck. She is only thinking about cars.

Evan, Ellie and Jesse are ready for the shop to open. Ring! Ring!
Ellie answers the phone. It's Mr. Roadrunner. He's at home with a
broken leg. He wants an ice cream cone with five scoops delivered to his
house. One ice cream cone coming right up!

Stop and Discuss

Evan scoops the ice cream and they are ready to go.
Well almost everyone... Molly's thoughts are still stuck on cars.
The fun stops and the other kids feel frustrated. If Molly wants to go,
she needs to think about the group plan.

Stop and Notice

While the kids are waiting for Molly, the ice cream begins to melt.
No one is thinking about the ice cream. They are all looking at
and thinking about Molly. Evan reminds her they have to go.
Molly wants to be part of the plan, so she agrees.

All the kids are excited to deliver the ice cream and
want to be first out the door. Only one person can be first.
Oh no! Everyone's thoughts are stuck on being first.

The kids push and shove. Everyone feels mad...and squished.
They are stuck, stuck, stuck. No one is having any fun.
Another scoop of ice cream melts.

Stop and Notice

Ellie wiggles free first and sits in the ice cream truck. Ellie wants to drive... but so does everyone else. "I want to be the driver!" yells Evan. "That's not fair," says Jesse. Only one person can drive the truck.

Oh no! Everyone's thoughts are stuck on being the driver. And now, the door is stuck too. Everyone feels upset. Evan pushes and pulls on the door. This is no fun! Another scoop on the ice cream cone melts away.

Finally, the other kids take a seat and Ellie begins to drive. Ellie thinks
Mr. Roadrunner's house is straight ahead. Jesse thinks it's to the left.
"Go this way, Ellie," he says as he points. "No, go this way!" yells Evan.
Molly thinks they need to turn around and go in the other direction.
"We're going the wrong way..." she calls out.

They can only drive in one direction. Oh no! Everyone's thoughts are stuck about which way to go. Ellie turns the wheel to the right...to the left... in a circle. And now their truck is stuck too. Everyone feels mad. What happened to the fun? There goes another scoop of ice cream from the cone.

After they work together and push the truck out of the sand, they finally arrive at Mr. Roadrunner's house. Mr. Roadrunner is waiting for his ice cream BUT... the kids see he has a really cool cactus garden. Evan gets close to see a woodpecker living inside a cactus. Jesse sniffs the cactus flowers. Molly and Ellie jump from rock to rock.

Everyone is thinking about the cactus garden and NOT
Mr. Roadrunner or his ice cream. Oh no! Everyone's thoughts are stuck on
the cactus garden. And now their clothes are stuck too. Ouch! Everyone
feels uncomfortable. The fun stops. And the last scoop on the ice cream
cone melts into a puddle on the ground.

Finally, the kids knock on Mr. Roadrunner's door. He opens the door and sees a group of children standing together. He notices they are all wearing aprons and hats. He makes a smart guess they are from the ice cream shop and have come to deliver his five scoop cone!

Then he sees... an empty cone.

Stop and Discuss

The kids notice that Mr. Roadrunner looks confused. Then they see he is looking at the empty ice cream cone. Wait... the **EMPTY** ice cream cone? The ice cream is gone! Oh no! Where did it go?

Mr. Roadrunner says, "I ordered a five scoop cone. What happened?"
The kids think about what did happen. They remember all the times they
got stuck in their thinking when the group plan was to deliver
the ice cream to Mr. Roadrunner.

Stop and Discuss

The kids tell Mr. Roadrunner they will be back with a five scoop cone. They need a plan.

Stuck thinking didn't work. The fun stopped, it took too much time, and the ice cream melted. Everyone felt upset.

They need to use *flexible* thinking. 'Being flexible' means we can think about what everyone needs, change our thinking and change our own or the group plan.

Stop and Notice

It's expected to use flexible thinking to be part of the group.
When we are flexible thinkers we can make different choices that
help us be part of the group plan.

Then everyone feels good.

The kids need to get back to the store. "I'll drive!"
"It's my turn!" I'm the driver now!" they all yell at the same time.
Uh oh, everyone wants to drive.

The kids stop and think. There can only be one driver at a time. When they all wanted to drive before, they got stuck. If they keep arguing about who will drive the truck, they will get stuck again.

Stuck thinking means the fun will stop and people will feel frustrated. Then they can't get another cone for Mr. Roadrunner.

But wait...

This time they can change their thinking and be flexible!

"Can I please be the driver this time?" asks Molly. Evan wants to drive, but remembers that getting stuck on an idea made the fun stop and the ice cream melt. He can be flexible! "Maybe I can drive next time," he says.

Ellie wants to drive, but she drove last time. She can change her thinking and be flexible. "It's expected to take turns with jobs," she tells herself. "Sure, you can drive this time!" she tells Molly.

Jesse wants to hurry back to the shop to get the new ice cream cone. He thinks about the group plan. "If I don't drive, it's okay, there are other jobs I can do!" he thinks. He is flexible too! "Okay Molly," he says.

That means Molly gets to be the driver. Finally she gets to drive!
Evan, Ellie, Jesse and Molly all feel happy to be on their way.

Molly thinks about all the different things you can do when you play ice cream shop. She didn't want to scoop, or take orders, or use the cash register. But there are lots of different jobs to do, like driving the truck, and she loves driving! Molly thinks she would like to learn to take orders too. Because she was flexible, Molly found out playing ice cream shop is fun! The kids head back.

Jesse scoops another cone and they're ready to go. Everyone starts racing for the door. But this time, they change their thinking and are flexible!

"I don't want to get stuck again," thinks Evan, "I can wait."
"It doesn't matter who is first," thinks Molly.

They all let Jesse go first and off they go to Mr. Roadrunner's house!

Evan tells the group, "I'll be the driver now!" "Okay!" says Ellie, "I already had a turn as the driver." Jesse says, "Sure, I got to be the ice cream scooper." Molly says, "I love driving, but it's your turn now. I can hold the cone instead."

Everyone is flexible about who gets to drive, so Evan jumps in the driver seat. Using flexible thinking gets them on the road quickly. None of the ice cream has melted. Everybody is feeling good.

Jesse remembers the way to Mr. Roadrunner's. Everyone is flexible and
follows Jesse's plan since he knows how to get there fast. This time they
don't get stuck arguing about which way to go. They have more time
for fun and sing songs together on the drive. None of the ice cream
has melted and everyone is happy.

Wow! The kids are already back at Mr. Roadrunner's house.
Using flexible thinking got them there quickly! They see his
fun cactus garden and still want to play.

Jesse is flexible. He looks at the cactus flowers and says to himself,
"First I need to deliver the ice cream, then I can smell the flowers"
as he keeps walking to the door.

Ellie and Molly think about jumping on the rocks, but use flexible thinking
and talk about playing together later. Evan sees the woodpecker in
the cactus. He wants to get a closer look, but stops and thinks about
the group plan. If he gets stuck, the ice cream will melt!
He is flexible and keeps walking.

All the kids are following the group plan to get
Mr. Roadrunner his ice cream. Everyone is feeling good!

Evan, Ellie, Jesse and Molly quickly put their bodies in a group and knock on Mr. Roadrunner's door. He opens the door to see the kids holding an ice cream cone with... five scoops! They used their flexible thinking!

Mr. Roadrunner thanks them for his ice cream. He feels happy about his cone and can see that the kids were flexible so they could work as part of a group and follow a group plan! The kids ask if they can look around his cactus garden. Mr. Roadrunner says, "Sure!" and reminds them to be careful not to get stuck on any of the cacti.

Now that Mr. Roadrunner has his ice cream, they go back to their shop. Using flexible thinking gives the group more time for fun. They were so quick to deliver the ice cream and get back to the shop, they have lots of time to play together and make giant delicious sundaes. Everyone is feeling great about being together and they love their ice cream treats!

...And they even have time to play together with Molly's cars.